Don't Punch People in the Junk:
(Seemingly) Obvious Life Lessons to Teach Kids

Kelly Wilson

For my husband and children, who encourage me to be my best self.

Table of Contents

Introduction

Parenting is by far the most challenging and rewarding endeavor I have ever attempted. I laugh at parenting because it's difficult - if I didn't laugh at it, then I would cry. And what my friend so lovingly calls my "truly horrible cry face" isn't attractive *per se* and wouldn't score me any new friends. However, my smile is - in a word – outstanding, so there's that.

I have two children, both boys, currently nine and six years of age, respectively. For the purpose of allowing my children to retain some measure of privacy as well as a shred or two of dignity, I call them Oldest and Youngest in this vulnerable and hilarious work of art regarding the journey of parenting; in addition, I call my husband, in the most complicated manner, Husband.

Each chapter represents a valuable lesson that I have learned regarding the obvious statements that we, as parents, must illustrate to our children so that they can navigate life. It is a chronological representation of the obvious life lessons our family experienced over a (roughly) two-year period, largely based on the children. A public diary of sorts, this book captures one of life's many dichotomies: raising children is often equal parts joy and delight mixed with maddening frustration and heartache.

Although many of the statements and lessons in this book seem like common sense, there may be several that you have already said or will someday say in the indeterminate future, all with the general air of amazement that you even need to utter the words out loud to another human being.

Many of these lessons involve statements that I never dreamed I would have to state directly to my children.

Lesson 1- Don't Punch People in the Junk if You Want Friends

February 2012

The phone calls from the principal of my kids' school began when Youngest was in the first grade. At that point, I had received phone calls from teachers and office staff regarding different issues, but not yet from the principal himself.

I had taught elementary school for about ten years altogether, leaving the profession to pursue a writing career while Husband continued to teach in our local school district. I have a special understanding of what it means to get a phone call from the principal regarding my children and their behavior.

"Everyone's fine," Mr. Principal began. "But I did have an interesting conversation this morning with Youngest."

Indeed, I thought. I couldn't figure out from his tone what the word "interesting" meant, exactly…but it couldn't be good. I rolled my eyes, anticipating a joke-gone-wrong on Youngest's part.

"A student reported that on the way home yesterday afternoon, Youngest hit him in the penis while they were riding the bus," Mr. Principal continued.

My face froze as I felt the guffaw build in my stomach and begin to travel upward. Red-faced, I clapped a hand over my mouth and pulled the phone away just in case some errant bubbles of laughter escaped.

God help me, I thought, *to not laugh in Principal's ear*. To my credit, I didn't think that our first official conversation would involve the word "penis." Like I said, I laugh so that I don't cry.

I paused, breathing deeply, shoving the guffaw back down into my midsection.

"Okaaaaay." I managed to speak just above a whisper.

"And this morning as school was starting," Mr. Principal continued, "he hit a different kid in the stomach, but it was pretty close to his private parts."

9

So basically, Youngest was involved in two separate incidents of hitting a kid in the privates within an 18-hour period. It seemed odd to me that Youngest couldn't go a full 24 hours without punching someone in the junk.

"That *is* interesting," I said.

"I sat with the children this morning to discuss both incidents," he said. "Youngest admitted to both with a refreshing honesty."

I supposed this was good news, as Youngest was creative with the truth on a regular basis.

"The first incident wasn't provoked, but the second issue was pre-empted by the child saying he didn't want to be Youngest's friend," Mr. Principal continued. "Youngest reviewed with me the different strategies he could have used to deal with the situation, so he knows what he should have done."

"Right," I said. Youngest was no dummy.

"So because of his choices, I'm going to have to give him an in-school suspension." Mr. Principal continued to explain the details while I wandered to the kitchen window, looking out at the street in front of our house.

I leaned my head against the window's cool glass once the conversation was over, beginning to feel my blood boil. A sense of helplessness started to sneak in.

What a surprise, I thought. *Punching people in the junk is not the way to make friends.*

Now, this seems obvious to me, so much so that I didn't ever consider that I would need to say these words out loud to any children, much less my own. It's not in the usual list of manners to teach, like *chew with your mouth closed* or *don't interrupt people in the middle of a conversation.*

Considering the long list of lessons that we end up having to teach our children, this thought occurred to me: Don't *all* of these rules just seem like plain old common sense?

When it comes down to it, there have been several life lessons that I was not prepared to teach my kids simply because they seem, well, obvious. And if I – a well-educated, cultured, intelligent mother of two – don't know about these (seemingly) obvious lessons that I'm apparently supposed to be teaching my kids, then there must be other parents out there, just like me.

There are times when I think Husband is a genius.

After the phone call with Mr. Principal ended, I fumed for the rest of the afternoon, wasting mental energy while coming up with zero viable solutions other than to wait for dinner. It's a personal and time-honored rule that *no decisions should be made on an empty stomach*, and dinnertime rapidly approached.

In the chaos of the kids arriving home from school, finishing homework and chores, speeding to and from piano lessons, and actually cooking dinner, there was little desire or time to have an in-depth discussion with Youngest anyway. So at the dinner table, Husband asked for details about the two junk-punching incidents.

Youngest recited the facts of the two events, and in light of what was essentially no new information, we ate in silence for a while.

"So," Husband finally said with a sigh. "You punched people after they said they wouldn't be your friend."

Youngest nodded, his blue eyes as wide and innocent as a pool of water on a sweltering day, its glassy surface hiding the hungry piranha swimming beneath.

"What could you have done instead?" I asked.

Youngest thought for a minute, slurping a spaghetti noodle before answering. "Ignore. Walk away. Tell an adult. Make a deal." He rattled off the answers as if he were reading them from a grocery list.

"So, you know what to do, you're just choosing not to do anything but punch people in their privates," I clarified.

He looked from me to Husband and back again, promptly stuffing a meatball into his mouth. He chewed slowly, clearly not wanting to participate in the conversation.

"Well, it appears that you are unable to make good choices for yourself," Husband said. "Which means that we will make all of your choices for you."

Hold up, I thought. This seemed like a lot of work…for *me*. After all, I didn't punch anyone in the junk.

"So we'll decide what you wear, what you eat and when…" Husband continued.

"Ah," I said with dawning understanding. "So I can tell him to pack whatever I want for his lunch, and choose his snack for him."

"And we pick out what he wears each day."

13

"And what he plays with!"

"Which means we need to clean out his room."

Youngest sighed. This was not the first time we had packed up his possessions, holding them ransom until we observed better behavior and choices.

"You know, Youngest," I said. "The only people who really have no self-control are babies. So I guess we'll treat you like a baby."

He sat, stoically slurping one spaghetti noodle at a time, considering the ramifications of these consequences. Which weren't incredibly clear until about a minute later.

"So we decide when you're done with dinner," Husband said, rising from the table and grabbing Youngest's plate. "And that time is now."

"What?" Youngest asked. "Wait!"

"Nope," said Husband. "We have toys to pack."

As Youngest helped Husband box up his toys for storage in the garage, I contemplated what I would have him pack for his lunch. I had a feeling it wasn't going to be a peanut butter and jelly sandwich. He did, after all, have leftover spaghetti and meatballs on

14

his plate from dinner – surely that would be fine covered in a film of

grease in the cold light of day?

Lesson 2 - Wear Your Shoes When You Leave the House

September 2009

In my experience, behavior patterns in children are pretty consistent from year to year. As a teacher, I never had a conference with parents who were completely surprised regarding what I had to say about their children, either positive or negative.

Therefore, it follows that Youngest's school behavior patterns didn't suddenly "happen" with the result of phone calls from the principal in first grade. His behavior patterns were evident from the day his formal education began.

"MOM!" my four-year-old cried out from the backseat. "I forgot my shoes."

16

"Wha-?" I said, driving into the preschool parking lot on a sunny Friday morning. It was his first official day of school and my first precious hours of freedom since giving birth to Oldest seven years before.

I flipped down the rearview mirror to see if Youngest was serious.

"My shoes, I forgot them." He smiled his charming, most Cheshire-cat grin. Yep, he was serious.

In the space of three seconds, my brain whirled with options as I parked the car. *Should we go get them? What about consequences – should he even be allowed to go to preschool today? I don't want to be THAT mean, it's his first day, he's so excited. Will they even let him in without shoes? Hey, what about my two and a half hours of freedom? Who leaves the house and forgets to wear SHOES?*

"Let's go," I said, opening his door, still unsure about what to do. Regardless of whether or not he would stay, I had to let Preschool Teacher know.

"But I don't want to get bit by a spider on the ground!" He stood, perched on the door frame, his toes curled around the edge.

"Should've thought about that before forgetting shoes," I said without sympathy. I strong-armed him out of the car and onto the pavement.

"Hi, how are yo – ," Preschool Teacher started to say as we walked into the classroom.

"He forgot shoes," I interrupted. Sweat dampened my forehead and my stomach tightened. Truly, it had been enough effort to get out the door on time this morning. Did I really need to remind my children to wear their shoes when they left the house?

I could only imagine the first impression that this incident was making.

To my surprise, Preschool Teacher smiled. "It's okay, we're not going outside."

"Oh," I said. "Okay." My shoulders, up to my ears with tension, gradually began to relax. I smiled at Youngest, gave him a kiss, snapped a few pictures of him without his shoes, and left, freedom intact.

As I drove out of the preschool parking lot, I resolved to look at Youngest's feet on a more regular basis. I had apparently failed to point out that shoes were necessary before leaving the house.

Lesson 3
It's Not the Teacher's Job to Wipe Your Butt

September 2009

It wasn't more than a week into the school year that I got The Look when I arrived to pick up Youngest from preschool.

I knew The Look because, as both a teacher and a parent, I had given it many times. The Look can communicate a variety of different messages depending on the specific situation, like *Cut it out*, *There's a problem*, *We need to talk*, and *Your kid's in trouble*.

I took a deep breath when Preschool Teacher caught my eye and gave me The Look. Youngest sat happily on his spot on the carpet, playing with another kid while waiting for me to pick him up. As Preschool Teacher approached, I tried to guess what had transpired during the morning – had Youngest hit another kid, had he hurled a toy at a classmate, had he thrown a fit?

"Hi, how are you?" Preschool Teacher asked.

"I'm okay," I said with a hesitant smile. "I gather there's a problem?"

"Well…" she hesitated, then continued in a loud whisper, "does Youngest wipe his own bottom at home?"

I stifled a choke and guffaw at the same time. My mouth twitched, and I forced the laughter down into my gut. This question, I did not expect.

"Ye-es," I said carefully, face flushing with the effort of controlling myself. "Why?"

"Oh, okay, well he's just testing me, then," Preschool Teacher whispered under her breath.

"What happened?" I asked.

"Youngest told me that he needed to use the bathroom, and as you can see it's right across the hall from our classroom." She pointed behind me to the restrooms. I had, in fact, used the girl's bathroom once, almost killing myself trying to use the undersized toilet. I thought at the time that perhaps they should just set the toilet bowls directly into the floor to avoid potential injury to adults.

"So I allowed him to go as it was the end of our bathroom break time anyway," she continued, "but he was in there awhile, maybe ten minutes."

Okay, I thought, *nothing unusual there*.

"Then I heard him yelling for me, 'Preschool Teacher! Preschool Teacher?' so I went to investigate. He was fine and everything, but as I stood outside the door to the bathroom he told me that it was time for me to..." she paused, forming air quotes with her fingers, "...'wipe his butt.'"

I covered my face with both hands and shook my head. I could sense the scandal of Youngest's use of the word "butt" instead of "bottom," which simply added insult to injury regarding the current wiping controversy.

I had no words. As a writer, this is rare.

After about ten seconds, I looked up, my face carefully blank (I think). "No," I said. "He is required to wipe his own butt at home." I refused to bow to the pressure to use the word "bottom."

"That's what I thought," Preschool Teacher said. "He's just testing me." Under the circumstances, she looked fairly unperturbed.

With a smile, she said goodbye to Youngest and we headed for the car.

"So how was preschool?" I asked as he climbed into his seat and put his seatbelt on.

"Good," he said. "We had raisins and Goldfish crackers for snack."

"Yum," I said. "I heard you went poop." I flipped down the rearview mirror to see his expression.

He looked back at me, matter-of-fact. "Yep."

"You know that Preschool Teacher doesn't wipe your butt." It wasn't a question. "Nobody wipes your butt…but you."

He looked at me steadily in the mirror, a challenge to this obvious social rule. I stared back, willing him to concede this point. For me, this was a deal-breaker.

He sighed, finally, and dropped his eyes. "Okay."

"Good," I said, starting the car. "Just so we're clear."

Lesson 4 – Deodorant is not for China

January 2010

Youngest's preschool schedule required that he accompany me on many shopping trips. Since I wasn't working steadily outside the home at the time, I was into couponing quite heavily, which required stopping at a few different stores throughout any given week to take advantage of sales and coupons.

One day while shopping, Youngest and I stood in line with our products in a basket. He had pushed the basket through each aisle that we visited, patiently waiting while I compared my coupons with the store advertisement with the "Is this the best price?" argument going on in my own head.

In line, his patience ran out, and he began taking the lids off the deodorants and sniffing them one at a time. Fortunately, each deodorant container had the safety cap that (I imagined) kept small children and dogs from eating it, because it's not enough to simply assume that this is an obvious rule.

"Do you wanna smell?" he asked, holding a stick of deodorant out to me.

"Mmmmm," I said, breathing deeply. "Smells like Daddy."

"No, it's for China," he said, matter-of-fact.

Wow, I thought. *I'm doing a great job at educating my young child about the globe. Imagine, a four-year-old who knows about China. Perhaps he's also mission-minded, through what he's learned at church or perhaps from my own heroic efforts at spiritual leadership.*

I was very proud of myself.

"Really?" I asked. "Deodorant is for China?"

"Yeah!" Youngest smiled. "Right?"

"I suppose," I said. "For all of the people who live there."

"People live there? In China?"

"Of course."

Youngest looked confused. "China is for moms!" he said.

"Well, China is for a lot of people."

"Can we go there?" he asked.

"Absolutely," I said. "You don't have to be a mom to go there." At this point, I could hear the angels in Heaven singing my praises, since I was such an excellent mother. "Men and women of all kinds can visit, even kids! Anyone can go to China."

"Wait," Youngest said. "What *is* China?"

Uh-oh. The angels abruptly fell silent.

"A really big country in Asia," I said. "People live and work there."

He looked confused for a moment. "No," he said. "China is for moms like you 'cause you don't have a penis."

Now it was my turn to be confused. *China*, I thought. I studied him as he continued to sniff the deodorant and I tried to figure out what my lack of a penis had to do with geography.

Understanding dawned. CHINA!

He wasn't saying "for China," he was saying "va-gina"- or, at the very least, "for gina," as in the last part of the word "vagina." This may have indicated a speech impediment of some kind.

And apparently Youngest picked up the idea somewhere that deodorant is for vaginas instead of armpits. This could be a problem.

I also abruptly realized the glaringly obvious - Youngest was not a citizen of the global community. I had, in fact, not been doing a stellar job teaching my children about the world.

"Actually, Youngest," I said, my cheeks pink and quite warm, "deodorant is not for China. At all."

He nodded. "What's it for?"

"Armpits."

He considered me thoughtfully, deciding whether or not to believe me.

"Seriously, it's for armpits," I said, giggling. "And don't eat it!" I added for good measure.

"Okay," he agreed with a smile. "It's for armpits!"

I made a mental note that Youngest refused to agree that deodorant is not, in fact, for eating.

Lesson 5 - You're Always a Great Parent... Until You Have Kids

February 2010

As a teacher, I observed a variety of parenting styles and the kids who did or did not benefit from them. Each year during my career, I filed away a few rules about what kind of parent I would be based on these observations.

For example, I would NEVER:

- Talk to the principal without talking first with a teacher about a problem, or otherwise be mean to a teacher

- Do my kids' projects for them, especially at the last-minute

- Feed my kids food from McDonald's, *especially* Happy Meals

- Play video games at home, or allow my kids to have video games

- Buy my children products, including books or toys, licensed by mainstream corporations featuring cartoon characters

- Berate or shame my children at a parent-teacher conference

- Get into everyone's "bidness" around the school, as in gossiping about other families, teachers, or administrators

- Bail my kids out by bringing them whatever they left at home, regardless of importance

Some of these "rules" are more important and serious than others, but the point was that I swore I would *never* be *THAT* mom, the ones constantly making excuses for their children. Kids need to face the consequences of their actions, positive or negative, to help them learn life's difficult lessons!

I was so good at parenting, *especially* before I had children.

When Oldest was in second grade, I got up one morning to make coffee. Next to the coffee pot, I discovered his Invention Project that he had left on the counter.

It was due that day.

I stared at it, deliberating. Should I take it to him at school? Or should he be out of luck?

Before I had kids, this wouldn't even have been an issue. *Let the kid suffer!* I would have said. But now…this was Oldest.

We have always called Oldest the Most Sincere Pumpkin in the pumpkin patch, which is a play on the idea from *It's the Great Pumpkin, Charlie Brown.* If there ever was a kid who would get visited by the Great Pumpkin based on pure sincerity of spirit, it would be Oldest.

The last time our house was ravaged by fevers and puking, he said to me, "Mom, you took care of me when I was sick last week, now I'm going to take care of you." And he did, graciously bringing me clear soda and saltine crackers, taking my temperature, and periodically checking the Puke Bowl by my bed.

Oldest is also a 40-year-old soul in a kid's body. Since he started kindergarten, Oldest set his alarm each night before bed, got up in the morning on his own, dressed, brushed his teeth, ate breakfast, fed the dog, packed his lunch and left for school on time, every time, *every single day.*

Which was partly why I had just gotten my bones out of bed and Oldest was already gone – it was time to wake Youngest and myself in order to get to preschool on time.

So when I saw his Invention Project on the counter, which was a cleaner-upper for kids that had a remote – all made from recycled cardboard and created without any input or help from me – I threw my rules out of the window.

I took the Invention Project down to the garage and put it in my car. After dropping Youngest off at preschool, I stopped by Oldest's classroom to bring him his project. Yep, I was *THAT* mom.

I was happy to say that he was appropriately embarrassed by his mom showing up at school. I felt pleased with my decision, so much so that I stopped by the store and picked up a couple of SpongeBob and Disney books, planned on taking them to McDonald's for Happy Meals for dinner to be followed by family video game time with the Wii. We'd probably have ice cream sundaes too, just for good measure.

Lesson 6 - Airport Security Requires a Flask

March 2010 (Referencing March 2008)

I collect flasks.

Believe it or not, I am not a drunk, nor am I in denial about being an alcoholic (the irony of that statement is that I'd say those things if I were a drunk, but never mind). Collecting flasks for me comes from an idea born from a trip I took to Africa several years ago.

I met a young woman who has since become a Best Friend of mine on that trip, and it's safe to say that we both struggled with culture shock during our time in Kenya.

One afternoon during our trip, Best Friend stood outside a village church after the Sunday service. She drank a cup of what our group leader lovingly called "Barnyard Chai," a combination of coffee freshly brewed over a brazier, mixed with milk that even ten minutes before had been sloshing around in the udder of a nearby cow or goat. Mix in some spices and a couple of pieces of random straw, and the drink is complete.

Best Friend visited with Kenyan church members, doing her best to communicate using a combination of hand gestures, limited Swahili, and English, all without spilling her drink. During one conversation, she calmly watched as a fly landed in her cup, struggled to get out, and eventually drowned in her chai.

Not wanting to seem ungrateful, she finished her drink and handed the cup back to our host, the fly lying dead in the dregs.

"So you didn't take the fly out?" I asked later.

"Nope," she answered.

"How did you drink it?" I asked. "I mean, there was a dead fly in your coffee."

"There's a valuable little phrase I repeat to myself sometimes," Best Friend said. "It is: *This is not me, I am not here.*"

This phrase stuck with me. I've lost track of how many times over the years I've repeated it silently to myself, finding a numb, distant, happy place for a few minutes while children are screaming or I feel that at any moment I may lose what's left of my sanity.

This is not me, I am not here is also the best description I can think of when it comes to why I collect flasks. I don't fill my flasks with alcohol and carry them around with me. I didn't one day wake up and decide that collecting flasks sounded like a great hobby for my station in life - a suburban mom who is raising a family, managing a household, driving a minivan, and working from home.

But when I found myself in situations where I felt the stress of all that is associated with parenting, I wanted some relief without scarring my children for life, and the only thing I could think of was to joke about having a flask. It's my own personal way of saying, *This is not me, I am not here.*

I began to qualify experiences that involved stress with names of flasks, such as *The Mall Flask. The Grocery Shopping Flask. The Funeral Flask.*

And *The Airport Security Flask.*

Husband is the band director at the local high school, so we trek with 50 or so kids and chaperones to Disneyland every other spring for a Band Trip. It may sound scary, but the trips are actually a lot of

33

fun. One year, we decided that our kids – ages 4 and 7 at the time – were ready to appreciate the trip, so we forked over the money for Oldest and Youngest to join us.

After four days in the purely ironically-named *Happiest Place on Earth*, I saw a sign for Blue Moon and declared I would give my right arm for a foamy 16-ounce plastic cup of temporary happiness. I began to plan the process – I would give my arm FIRST, then enjoy the foamy fruits of my labor and alleviate the stress of the trip. Then one of my best friends – who, consequently, supplied me with many of the more unusual flasks in my collection – reminded me that I'm right-handed and should probably give my left arm.

In a fit of *This is not me, I am not here*, I began to search for a Disneyland-themed flask. I scoured every store throughout Disneyland itself, Downtown Disney and California Adventure to find the Mickey Mouse-shaped flask of my dreams.

It was, however, not to be found. Curiously, I found shot glasses emblazoned with Disney logos of various kinds, which I thought was just as incriminating and, frankly, as strange as a Disney-themed flask would be.

There was, of course, no drinking on a school trip, and I wouldn't break that rule; but clearly, I was ready to leave.

So it was with varying degrees of relief that I found myself with two young children navigating airport security at LAX. We stood in line together while Husband steered the fifty or high school students plus chaperones through the airport check-in and security process.

This left me in line with Oldest (seven years old), Youngest (four years old), a medium-sized stuffed Dumbo, my (rather large) purse, my carry-on bag, two small suitcases, three boarding passes and Youngest's backpack, shuffling toward the buckets and conveyor belt that was airport security.

Not to worry, though – there was no rush. The line toward the security bays was easily 100 yards long, so there was plenty of time to stand and wait with two children who attempted to climb the walls and their suitcases while I tried to ensure that they didn't fall and break their heads open on the incredibly hard cement and linoleum floor. I don't "do" blood, and I couldn't take the idea of spending hours in the local emergency room while someone got stitches in his head and I retched in the corner while mumbling, "Dear God can't we just go home…"

I took a deep breath. *Airport security requires a flask*, I thought. I began to imagine the logistics required to take a flask in a carry-on bag through security and onto an airplane. The flask would have to be plastic, perhaps made from recycled material, and hold no more than 3.4 ounces of sweet sanity-giving nectar. Three ounces would be plenty.

After about thirty minutes of imagining my Airport Security Flask, deep breathing, and chanting, *I am not here*, we approached the security section with the bins and x-ray machines. Depending on how we were funneled through the line, we would have to take the stairs or the escalator, which loomed ahead with its grooved, gray metal steps unfolding magically out of the floor and levitating passengers up to the floor above.

We were directed toward the escalator, of course the most obviously dangerous of the two options. I pushed Oldest in front of me, reminding him to keep both feet on the step. He joyfully took off while I climbed onto a step, holding Youngest's sticky, sweaty hand and, might I reiterate, carrying a medium-sized stuffed Dumbo, my (rather large) purse, my carry-on bag, two small suitcases, three boarding passes and Youngest's backpack.

Youngest suddenly let go of my hand and stood, frozen with indecision. I ran the risk of hurting him by making him fall on those evil-looking metal grooves of the escalator stairs or leaving him behind. I let go of his hand and watched helplessly as he considered each step as it appeared from the floor, a hypnotizing, circular ballet.

"It's okay, buddy," I called. "Just take a step and it will carry you."

He stared as each step appeared, clearly wanting to figure out how it worked, perhaps by sitting down and taking it apart like one of his toys at home.

"Just take a step and come up," I called again.

I could tell he heard me and had chosen to ignore me – he almost waved my voice away, as if he needed time to think. I stood, frozen on my step, two-thirds of the way up the escalator when I could see him make a decision.

"No," I said, loudly. My voice echoed off the cement floors and high ceilings.

"NO!" I said, louder.

He turned around and prepared to sit down on the metal steps.

"No! No! NO! NO!" I screamed, now at the top of the escalator. I dropped everything and prepared to vault down to the bottom to save Youngest.

Thankfully, air travel being what it is today, airport security people can move FAST. Three people in uniform appeared and stood Youngest up, scowling up at me and loading him onto an escalator step while fellow travelers stared.

When he arrived at the top, I hugged him fiercely, mentally kicking myself for forgetting the *most important preparation that I should have made* for this trip.

Forget packing snacks. Forget portable DVD players or laptops or toys to play with on the plane. Don't waste your time explaining the finer points of Disneyland lines and rides or planning a rough budget for your trip.

Instead, teach your kids how to safely ride an escalator. And clearly, both Airport Security and Disneyland require a flask.

Lesson 7 - Moms aren't the Only Ones Who Need Prozac

April 2010

There are a few acronyms and accompanying conditions in our home that feel like a conspiracy engineered by the pharmaceutical companies. There's some ADHD and PTSD, along with your basic depression and/or anxiety among one or two physical ailments that are spread across our family members.

After Youngest was born, I lapsed into a sea of Post-Partum Depression so deep that I thought I might drown. My counselor wisely suggested that I try an anti-depressant.

For my own sanity and for the health of my family, I agreed, which has been a beneficial move for all of us, including our pets.

Pat the Cat lived to be slightly more than fifteen years old. We adopted her and her sister Smokey the week after Husband and I got married. Pat had been through living in an apartment, then two different houses, the arrival of our first dog, both Oldest and Youngest as tail-pulling toddlers, the death of the first dog, her sister Smokey running away, the new puppy Gilly (our second dog), and the adoption of Pepper the kitten.

By the time she turned fifteen years of age, Pat was perturbed by the changes and additions to our household. Plus, in an effort to find a better and less-pain-in-the-butt cat litter box, I bought a new one. In context, that was a mistake.

Soon after Pepper the kitten came along, different parts of the house began to smell of cat pee. I knew it was Pat, since both Husband and I had actually witnessed her choose a pile of our clean clothes, climb to the top, clear a spot and deposit a healthy dose of her most vile-scented urine.

Cat pee is by far the worst scent in the history of the earth, and one I do not want in my house. More importantly, I began to worry.

Pat was, simply put, old. I began to wonder if she was too old to get up and down to the stairs to the litter box or if something was wrong with her kidneys. Had she lost weight? Can cats get diabetes? Could she have leukemia?

I avoided the whole thing for a while, and then I could no longer stand finding pockets of urine-scented laundry. I made an appointment with The Vet.

When we arrived, I was quite stressed, partly from Pat's yowling on the trip over, which only continued when I took her out of the carrier and placed her on the cold, stainless steel table.

While I watched, The Vet gave Pat a thorough exam. "She looks great," she said, even as Pat growled and tried to bite her hand.

"Really?" I asked. My shoulders slumped in relief.

"Yeah, she's in really good shape. However, the peeing everywhere has to stop."

I heartily agreed, and we decided that The Vet needed to take a blood panel to try and figure out what was going on. If nothing was physically wrong, then it was a behavior issue.

Later that evening, The Vet called with the results of the test. "This is the best cat I've ever seen on paper," she said.

"What? Really?"

"Yeah, especially for her age."

"That's wonderful!" I said. "But – "

"Yeah, the peeing needs to stop," the Best Vet in the World said. "So here's what I'm thinking, I'd like to put her on -"

At this point, I'm thinking a behavior plan. A vitamin. Some kind of "old cat" supplement.

Wrong on all counts.

"I'd like to put her on Kitty Prozac."

I flung the phone away from my face and laughed a guffaw that would wake the dead. Husband looked at me with alarm from where he sat in the living room.

"I'm sorry!" I said into the phone in between giggles. "That was totally not on my radar! It does, however, make perfect sense."

The Vet seemed delighted with how entertained I was by the Kitty Prozac. "I don't know what's in the stuff that redirects cats' behavior in this area, but it works. Keep her on a couple of months and then wean her off...although, some people never take their cats off the stuff. I mean, it's so cheap."

"And helpful," I said.

After more giggling and arrangements for me to pick up a ten-day sample and prescription, I hung up, satisfied that I wouldn't have to clean up random cat pee around my house much longer.

And once I thought about it for a while, with all of the stuff Pat had gone through, was it really any wonder that any or all of our pets would require medication?

Lesson 8 - Keep Your Pants on in Public

September 2010 (Referencing April 2010)

Dear God, please let Youngest keep his pants on.

This, on the first day of kindergarten, was my prayer.

Other moms, whose children kept their clothes on in public, wept as they passed by me on their way out the front doors of the school. I sat in the office, silently repeating my prayer while filling out Youngest's immunization record.

The issues with Youngest and his pants began during the first spell of warm weather the previous spring. I arrived early one afternoon to pick him up from preschool, when I again received The Look from the teacher as I approached.

Preschool Teacher stood by the edge of the playground, watching the preschoolers shriek with joy while they ran and played.

Sighing, I asked, "How's it goin?"

44

"Well," she said, "we've got a problem."

Preschool Teacher tried to speak softly even as the giggles and playful screams made it virtually impossible to hear her. The children were blowing off steam while waiting for their parents, chasing each other around in the dappled shadows from the leaves rustling in the breeze and sunshine. The playground was well-equipped, with monkey bars, a play structure with a slide, a couple of climbing toys, and a swing set situated in the far corner.

Apparently it was in this shady corner that Youngest had decided to shed his clothing. Perhaps he felt he needed additional vitamin D to make up for the long, cloudy winter, or maybe he was overheated.

 Probably not.

"Apparently Youngest and a couple of others were playing in that corner." Preschool Teacher pointed behind the swing set. "And he dropped his pants and declared, 'Get a load of my pot-o-gold.'"

In her seriousness, Preschool Teacher uttered the "pot-o-gold" phrase in words clipped by what I hoped was smothered amusement, but was probably just anger. And this made the words that much more hilarious.

I turned away, simultaneously horrified and entertained. In all fairness, it was just after St. Patrick's Day, and the preschool class had spent some time studying the legends involving leprechauns, rainbows and pots of gold. However, he must have gotten confused regarding how the whole "pot of gold" situation actually works, because he isn't preceded – or followed - by rainbows that settle at his nether regions.

Attempting to breathe normally and project the stony exterior of expected outrage, I inhaled deeply once…twice…a third time. When I felt like I could speak again, I turned back to face Preschool Teacher.

Thankfully, she spoke first. "I explained to him that his behavior was totally inappropriate, and if he did it again, we would need to sit down and have a meeting, all of us."

I nodded, the laughter still threatening but now underscored by the slow burn of anger. I wanted to explain so badly that we wear clothes at home, that I require my children to keep their clothing on in public *and* private, and that I felt totally mystified as to how Youngest could think that this kind of behavior would be acceptable.

But I didn't say it – I couldn't say anything.

As I helped Youngest in the car, I wondered what to say to him about the situation, or if anything I said could make an impact. Mostly, I was amazed that we needed to have this conversation at all.

"Dude," I said as Youngest got in the car. I crouched down so that he could look directly into my eyes while attempting to buckle his seatbelt. "Keep your pants on in public. This is basic information."

That is how I came to sit in the office on the first day of kindergarten, repeating *Please God, let Youngest keep his pants on all year.* As I repeated my mantra, I was surprised as the only other mother who was NOT weeping came and sat down next to me. Her little boy and Youngest had struck up a friendship during Kindergarten Orientation the day before, and she made sure that they were sitting together for this important official first day of school.

Youngest was nervous, so I profusely thanked her, telling her that I was also nervous, and about the whole pants issue.

She laughed. "Usually," she said, "my son says 'Look at my chicken nuggets!'"

Yes! I thought. *I'm not the only one! Perhaps I don't need to pray so hard...*

"Although, he hasn't ever taken his pants off at school," she added.

I smiled and nodded, silently repeating *Please God, let Youngest keep his pants on.*

Lesson 9 - Phonics are Not Always Fun

October 2010

"Well, I'm happy to report that Youngest has kept his pants on so far!" Kindergarten Teacher exclaimed. Husband, Oldest, Youngest and I sat around the outside edge of the teacher's kidney-shaped table, perched on a set of those undersized chairs found in primary classrooms. I almost fell off my chair in shock, but also because I was precariously perched with only one of my cheeks on the surface of the seat.

Those chairs are dangerously small.

Considering my prayer as school began, the fact that Youngest had kept his pants on in public was very good news. However, it was only mid-October: Conference Day.

The feedback from both Youngest's and Oldest's teachers simply got better from there. This particular Conference Day was one of those where I felt like all of our parenting diligence was paying off in ways that we could now see. However, neither child has hit any hormonal stages yet, so this could change literally at any moment.

Husband and I were also informed in both conferences that Youngest and Oldest are both doing incredibly well in reading. This, I've realized, can be both a blessing and a curse.

After both conferences were completed, we stopped by the Book Fair, which served as one of the school's main fundraisers for the library. As a proponent of public education and a lover of all books everywhere, I generously support the school's Book Fair each year. Youngest and Oldest, in the limits of a budget, chose a few books to purchase and bring home. Youngest chose a set of Spongebob phonics books right at his level.

While I did the dishes later that evening, I listened to both children reading different parts of their books to one another at the kitchen table. I didn't pay too much attention until I heard Youngest sounding out "SH" and "T".

Oh dear, I thought.

"SSSHHHH," Youngest labored over the sounds. "T-T-T. SSHH…TTT."

What kind of words do they have in those phonics books, anyway? I was starting to panic, trying to figure out how to redirect his attention without scarring him for life when it came to either reading or SpongeBob.

"That's not right," Oldest said, interrupting the dangerous phonics episode unfolding at the table.

"Why?" Youngest asked.

"You need a vowel!" Oldest insisted.

"What?" Youngest asked.

"A vowel! You can't just have SSSHHHHH and T-T-T, you have to have a letter in between."

"Like what?"

"I dunno, like A or E," Oldest said. Then in all innocence, he suggested, "Try I."

I held my breath, washing one particular pan for now the third time. *Not I, not I, not I,* I whispered to myself.

"OK," Youngest said, "SSSHHH -"

"HEY!" I yelled in that crazy cheerful tone when you're trying to cover something up. "You guys want a snack?"

"YEAH!" they yelled.

Youngest closed the book.

Crisis averted.

For now.

While Youngest's conference was positive overall, Kindergarten Teacher expressed some concerns. While Youngest was a great reader for his age, he wasn't so focused when it came to a few basic skills, like completing work. Coloring. Writing his name. Following directions. Sitting at a table.

You know, basic structure. Maybe he was so focused on my instruction to simply keep his pants on during the school day that he couldn't concentrate on anything else.

After the conference with Kindergarten Teacher, it was clear that something more intentional on my part needed to be done to help him adjust to the rigors of the kindergarten academic landscape. So off we headed to the nearest teacher store to find materials that might challenge and train him and add structure to our afternoons once he arrived home from Morning Kindergarten.

I was looking for a good book to help Youngest practice writing. He seemed to be struggling with that area in particular, having written "I like to go to the bathroom" in response to the Martin Luther King Jr. project they had been working on the week before. Did he not understand the "I Have a Dream" concept of the assignment, or was he simply not comfortable with printing his letters? Or was he distracted by a full bladder?

All good questions, with no answers.

I thought that getting him more comfortable with printing his letters might help, along with some freewriting practice and lessons in following directions.

Youngest was totally into this whole process. We looked at books together, flipping through them and talking about what we liked. As I browsed one side of the aisle, he read the titles of different books on the other side.

"Kin-der-gar-ten sssss-uuuuu-cccckkkkkk-ssss," I heard him read behind me.

What the - , I thought in confusion.

53

"Kin-der-gar-ten sssss-uuuu–cccckkkk–sssss," he said, much louder this time.

My jaw clenched. *What does he think he's doing?* I spun around, getting ready to speak quite loudly to Youngest in the middle of the teacher store.

"OH!" I yelled instead, realizing that he was trying to read the title of a workbook. "I believe that title is Kindergarten *Suc-cess*."

"Kin-der-gar-ten suc-cess!" he repeated, his finger tracing the words on the book cover.

"Yeah!" I said. He moved on to read other titles, while I searched for a book to teach him how to sound out words with more than one syllable. He could clearly use the practice.

Lesson 10 - Dry Humping is not for the Family Picture

November 2010

It was a Thanksgiving weekend when, during a visit to my mother-in-law's, we gathered for a traditional family portrait.

Every couple of years, the great-grandparents, mother-in-law, brother-in-law and his family, and our family of four all squish together at a local retail portrait studio in order to help create this timeless work of art.

In total, there were eleven of us shoved into the back corner of what would more appropriately be called the Portrait Closet, instead of Studio. We crammed into one end of a space about the size of my home's 1970s-style bathroom. The walls were black, the carpet was dark, and the lights were close and bright.

The two photographers were well-prepared and set us up in traditional poses – what else can you really do with eleven people? – and as quick and helpful as they were, the room was tiny.

Narrow.

Stifling.

Hot.

Beads of sweat began to run down my back as I stood squished among our crowd, an admittedly fantastic smile frozen onto my face.

Click Click

The photographers checked the screen, muttering to each other and giving us direction.

"Okay boys, we need smiles from each of you. Oldest, we need you to keep still."

Click Click

"Oops, someone closed their eyes."

Click Click

"Youngest, don't stick your tongue out."

At about the third pose, we were all getting just a tiny bit cranky.

In one pose, I stood on the middle right, slightly behind Mother-In-Law with Brother-In-Law on my left and Husband on my right. I felt pressure on my behind, and assumed it was Husband. Then I felt a slight gyrating sensation against my right hip. I was hot, sweaty, impatient, and I couldn't take it.

"HUSBAND IS DRY HUMPING ME RIGHT NOW!" I announced to the room.

Husband froze. The photographers' mouths gaped open. Mother-In-Law stared straight ahead, not turning to look at me or her son who had, just moments ago, dry humped me during the family photo for which she was paying good money.

Out of the corner of my eye, I could see my brother-in-law shaking with suppressed laughter and I could hear tiny giggles erupting from my teenage nephews.

That was all I needed. I started laughing, and so did everyone else. Giggling, I said, "Well, he was."

The next couple of photos after that were of family members, relaxed and smiling, and Husband standing ever so slightly away from me.

Though the result was an excellent family picture, you might not want to quote my exact words. Usually saying something strange, like "naked penguin" or "poopy pizza" will do the job – basically, if you put the word "naked" with any other word, you can A) get people's attention or 2) make people laugh. Other words like "butt" and "fart" also work nicely.

Now, before you judge me too harshly, know that I realized almost immediately that my 14-year-old and 12-year-old nephews heard what I said, as well as Oldest and Youngest. I was chagrined, and fearful of the stories my sons will one day tell their therapists (or Oprah) about me. I apologized to them later, stating – quite obviously, mind you - that they shouldn't say something like that in public.

My only other regret is that the photographer didn't snap a picture right when I said it so that I could see my mother-in-law's face, because apparently it was *priceless*.

Lesson 11 - Wipe Your Butt Before Your Parents Go Insane

January 2011

After the whole Kindergarten Sucks conversation, we settled into a new routine. Youngest went to Morning Kindergarten, came home, had lunch, played a game or read a story, and then he worked on a page out of each of his workbooks. I began volunteering at school, spending part of three mornings a week in his classroom, helping out in general and maintaining a presence specifically.

For the most part, this seemed to be working well – you'd think so, right?

Not so much. The month we started this new routine, he was written up an additional two times by his teacher. I began to wonder if they suspended kindergarteners at his school. I called the school counselor to schedule an appointment, wondering just how bad of a mother I might be.

The run-ins between Youngest and me continued at home as well. One afternoon, I said, "Youngest, I need you to get the mail for me. Would you do that please?"

His response – "No." (As a side note, he had been trying that response out, trying to be funny. I told him repeatedly that it was decidedly *not funny*).

"Let me rephrase," I responded. "Go get the mail please."

"No," he said, matter-of-fact. "I'm not going to do that."

I felt my blood pressure accelerate so fast that I became light-headed and thought I was going to pass out.

"Youngest. Come here," I said, my voice low and quiet, my words short and clipped. "I use questions and manners as a courtesy. GO. GET. THE. MAIL."

We stared at each other, unblinking, for a long moment. He relented. I took a deep breath, trying to slow my heart rate. Clearly, obedience wasn't his thing.

The very next morning, getting ready for school was quite rough due in part to the obedience issue, but mostly because Youngest needed to poop when he got up.

I don't have a problem with a morning poop *per se*, but Youngest takes a notoriously LOOOOOOONNNNNGGGG time to finish. Then he neglects to wipe his butt, doesn't flush and leaves the seat up.

So it's a lot of management for me, *especially* first thing in the morning.

Fifteen minutes later, he finally finished the pooping process itself. This left twenty minutes before the bus was scheduled to pick up Oldest and Youngest and deliver them to school.

"Did you wipe your butt?" I asked.

"Huh?" He stared at me as if this concept is completely foreign.

"I take it the answer is no," I said. "Go wipe it."

"Okay." Youngest disappeared into the bathroom, where he stayed for *ten minutes* while I dealt with getting myself ready and listening to Oldest, the resident Morning Person in our household, cheerfully chattering away.

"Did you wipe your butt?" I called from the kitchen, noting that there were ten minutes left before the bus came.

"I'm trying," he called out.

Not believing him, I headed for the bathroom. "What are you doing?"

He stood beside the toilet – which was still unflushed - in front of the toilet paper, rolling it around and around in its holder as if he'd never seen it before.

At this point, I really thought I was going to have some kind of stress-induced episode. My heart thumped and I could feel my blood boiling. My head started to ache and I saw tiny black spots at the edges of my vision.

And I wanted a flask of something to add to my morning coffee, because the caffeine alone just wasn't cuttin' it.

Not able to breathe, I said fairly loudly through clenched teeth, "WIPE YOUR BUTT BEFORE I GO INSANE." Then I ripped off some toilet paper, thrust it in his direction, and stared at him.

"What?" Youngest asked, starting to fidget.

Our eyes locked. He slowly reached out to grasp the toilet paper between his thumb and forefinger. It fluttered in the breeze created by my raspy deep breathing, trying to remain calm.

Finally, his gaze fell, and he crushed the toilet paper into one of his sweaty, five-year-old fists. Thrusting the glob of paper behind him, he wiped, throwing it into the toilet, flushing it, and putting the seat down as instructed.

"Now get dressed," I said, following him to his room.

With one minute to spare – and no breakfast – he got his coat and backpack on and headed out the door.

I had to laugh about it...or I would drown in my own tears. Or go insane – whatever works.

Lesson 12 - Centerfolds Happen to Kids

February 2011

You never really know what your children will love as they grow and develop, or what hobbies they will embrace to help them become the people they are meant to be.

A love of music and reading are passions we've instilled in both Oldest and Youngest since before birth – they both read above grade level and joyfully play several instruments.

But they also have developed a love for animals, real and stuffed, wild and domestic, large and small. It wouldn't surprise me if Oldest became a veterinarian.

And in that particular passion, during his second grade year, Oldest discovered the magazine *Cat Fancy*, and its related website *Cat Channel*.

At first, I had to pay no money and felt no obligation to aid in the development of this hobby. Oldest had a dealer for back issues of *Cat Fancy* - his piano teacher. After his lesson each week, Piano Teacher offered an additional *Cat Fancy* magazine to add to his collection as a reward for a job well done.

These tattered issues, sometimes with pages missing, were like gold to Oldest. He would hold each one lovingly to his chest as he received it, then cut out the pictures of different cats and tape them to a wall in his room – I called this The Cat Wall.

However, the back issues eventually ran out, and I began to hear on a pretty consistent basis about Oldest's desire for his own subscription to *Cat Fancy* magazine.

Once I discovered a special subscription deal for $12 for the entire year, who was I to turn it down and squelch my son's hobby? At $1 a month, this magazine subscription was a great deal, so I signed him up.

He waited impatiently for the delivery of his first *Cat Fancy* magazine, running to the mailbox each afternoon, only to be greeted with disappointment. He frowned as he handed me the rest of the mail, as he anticipated his magazine's delivery for what seemed like an eternity.

Until, triumphantly, Oldest ran up the stairs one afternoon waving the magazine with a cover photo of a white cat in the *Cats and Dogs* style of Mr. Tinkles from the movie, *Cats & Dogs* – long-haired, smushed face, angry eyes, and adorable.

"Caaaattt Faaaannnncccyyy's here!" Oldest yelled, holding the magazine aloft, striding around the living room like Vanna White showing off an incredible prize. "Wanna see?"

He had obviously already flipped through it as he walked between the mailbox and our living room. "Sure," I said, hand out.

"Hey, I want to see too," Husband said from the kitchen.

"You gotta wait," I said.

The magazine naturally flipped open to the center spread, these obviously more valuable pages, thicker in texture and weight than the rest of the publication. *Must be a poster to add to The Wall of Cats in his room*, I thought.

Pictured on this two-page spread was the white cat from the cover, laid out in all (her? his? its?) glory, luxuriously posing for the camera in a wide-angled shot that spanned the width of what was clearly a...centerfold.

"Whoa," I said, rotating the magazine.

"What?" Husband asked, looking over my shoulder. "Whoa! That's...well, a...a centerfold," he whispered.

"What's the big deal?" Oldest asked.

"Nothing," I said. "It's just quite a picture here of the Mr. Tinkles cat."

"Oh, yeah, I'm going to hang that poster on my wall!" Oldest grabbed the magazine and headed for his room.

Husband and I exchanged a look.

"You know, that makes me want to sing a little song," he said.

"Oh yeah?"

"You know, that *Centerfold* song from the '80s? I think it was by The J. Geils Band."

I grinned. "We'd have to change the words. It could be something like -

> *Not just a pet*
> *My cat is earning a paycheck*
> *My kitten is a centerfold*
> *(My kitten is a centerfold)."*

67

Husband laughed. "Don't forget the nah-nah part: *Meow, meow, meow-meow-meow-meow…*"

We sang the rest together:

"*Meow, meow, meow,
meow-meow-meow-meow-meow
mmmeeeoooowww!
(two-three-four…)*"

The tune instantly caught on. As Youngest sat on the edge of Oldest's bed, watching him tape new photo posters to The Cat Wall, they both absently meowed the chorus to *Centerfold*.

"Oh dear," I said to Husband.

"What? They don't know the real lyrics," he said.

"And they won't."

"But why not let them enjoy their innocent meowing?" he asked. "It's inspiring." With a thoughtful look, he headed down to the basement, and our collection of musical instruments.

The next day, Youngest needed to take something to share for Show and Tell. He chose Husband's newest musical creation: twenty seconds of the chorus to *Centerfold*, meowed into a digital recorder – in four parts - and burned onto a CD.

Lesson 13 – Some Things are Just Not That Big a Deal

March 2011

Husband, Oldest, Youngest and I spent the better part of a Saturday morning at the local Spring Fun Fair.

True to its marketing message, this fair really was fun – a lot of free stuff for the kids, coupons, demonstrations, fair food, $5 bike helmets, and a surprising number of spinning wheels with a variety of associated prizes. You know, like the Wheel of Fortune, only much smaller, standing upright on tables, and made of painted plywood and heavy-duty Styrofoam.

We strolled around the maze of booths, picking up stickers, candy, coloring books for the kids, and spinning as many of those wheels as we could.

It was at an insurance company booth that we stopped so the boys could complete some kind of throw-the-ball-game in order to receive a prize. Not to be outdone by the adjacent businesses, this booth also had a wheel to spin.

While Youngest and Oldest completed their game, another Insurance Guy at the booth moved the spinner from the table top to the floor so that Awesome Wheelchair Boy could reach it.

Awesome Wheelchair Boy was a kid of about ten years of age who rolled up to the spinner in a tricked-out wheelchair. While I couldn't describe the chair exactly, I remember supple black leather, chrome detail, and velvet cushions, while on the back a prominently displayed bumper sticker said HARDCORE SITTING.

Awesome Wheelchair Boy leaned over slightly and reached out a hand gloved in fingerless, black leather to give the wheel a spin while Youngest and Oldest came over to see what he would win.

The colors of each section of the spinner blurred as the wheel clacked around and around. This spinner had at least twenty slots with a wide variety of different prizes for participants to win. Seriously, *twenty*. Examples of possible prizes included gift cards to area coffee shops and restaurants, stationery sets, tickets to a concert, footballs, candy bars, and more.

The prizes spun in a dizzying array, around and around, slower and slower, the wheel click-click-clicked to a stop on…

Pedometer.

I stared at the spinner in disbelief. *Pedometer?*

My breath caught in my throat. *No*, I thought, during that miniscule moment of shared awkward silence when everyone involved knows that something could go terribly wrong. Plus, as a (albeit, dysfunctional) way to deal with my own discomfort, I was afraid that I was going to start laughing, which I felt that, under the circumstances, would be highly inappropriate.

"What's a pedometer?" Youngest yelled.

"Shhh," I said, trying to be inconspicuous, but also noting how much Youngest's reading had improved since the beginning of the school year.

In that moment, Insurance Man looked at Awesome Wheelchair Boy, the spinner, and the prizes stored in the stacked totes behind him.

God bless Insurance Man – he didn't miss a beat. "Would you like a pedometer, or would you like a football?" he asked Awesome Wheelchair Boy. The football prize was right next to the pedometer prize on the spinning wheel.

"I'd like a pedometer, please," Awesome Wheelchair Boy said. Taking his prize, he rolled to the next booth.

"But what's a pedometer?"asked Oldest.

"It's like a watch, only instead of telling what time it is, it tells you how many steps you take as you walk throughout the day," Husband explained.

Oldest and Youngest looked at Husband, then turned to look after Awesome Wheelchair Boy. Both kids wore expressions of concentration, eyebrows drawn and lips pursed. I could see that they were approaching a conclusion.

Oldest arrived first. "But he's not walking."

"Nope," I answered. "He's in a wheelchair."

"Well, that's not really a fair prize," Oldest said as we continued strolling through the veritable fair of fun. "I would have been mad."

"I can appreciate that," I said. "But do you think that winning a pedometer is the most difficult thing he'll have to face in his life?"

Oldest turned to look back at where Awesome Wheelchair Boy had gone. "No."

"Nope," I said. "At this point, it's probably not that big a deal."

"What will he do with the pedometer?"

"I'm not sure," I said. "Maybe give it as a gift or find another use for it."

I have no clue as to how he used it after he left the Spring Fun Fair, but it's during times of stress or disappointment in my own life that I remember Awesome Wheelchair Boy – I still wonder what he did with the pedometer.

Lesson 14 – Put Everything in its Place

April 2011

I really like Easter, for two main reasons:

- A) Jesus rose from the grave and showed Death what was

what and that's awesome and

- #2) Ham

Ham isn't your run-of-the-mill meat. Richer cousin to bacon, ham takes center stage at our house, much like the turkey from *A Christmas Story*.

Ham is perfect for Easter Sunday, with leftovers scarfed for as many days as they happen to last. Ham, like bacon, can improve the taste of *many* foods.

My local grocery store happens to traditionally have a great sale on ham the week before Easter, generally priced at $.99 cents a pound.

Anticipating Easter dinner, I gathered my shopping list and canvas bags and headed to the store, Youngest in tow.

There were quite a few items on my list, and to keep busy, Youngest was playing a game where he would stand in one spot at the front of the basket each time it stopped and reach for items on nearby shelves. Then he would pretend to put them into the cart and I would say, "Hey, dude, whatcha doin?" and we would both laugh.

This may sound annoying, but it was a nice break from the never-ending stream of questions he usually asks me while I'm juggling a grocery list, coupons, and deals during a shopping trip.

I remember approaching the ham. I remember reading the label. I can envision the ham in my cart.

The rest is a blank.

All I know is that I got home, analyzed my receipt, and found no evidence that I had actually bought the ham, nor was the ham in my car or my house.

So where had the ham gone?

No idea.

I turned to the one place the rest of those from my generation turn when diving into the depths of life's mysteries – Facebook. I received many worthwhile suggestions, but none that rang true. I must have just simply neglected to buy the ham.

Later that same night, I returned to the same store and found the same ham in the same place. This time, I actually put it in my cart, paid for it, and brought it home.

Rather large, the precious ham took up the bottom shelf of the fridge where I needed to store vegetables (when I actually bought them), so I asked Oldest to put it downstairs in the fridge in the laundry room. That was the Thursday before Easter.

Fast forward to Sunday morning, when I asked Husband to go down to the laundry room and retrieve the all-important and much-anticipated ham.

"There's no ham down there," he said, coming back upstairs.

Oh no, not again! I thought. *Why can't I hold on to this stupid ham?*

After further investigation, we found the ham. On my kitchen floor. In the bag. Where it had sat. For three days.

Oldest, who had helped in the Ham Investigation, stared at me in terror. "Oh, Mom. Oh, I'm sorry," he said. "Mom, Mom, Mom."

I stared at him, trying to make my face a blank and halt the stroke my body was threatening to have over this stupid ham. True, I had asked him to put the ham downstairs and true, he had neglected to actually follow through. But I couldn't help but conclude that he was involved in a much larger Ham Conspiracy set against me by the Universe.

"It's fine," I said. I hugged him as I saw tears threaten to fall from his eyes. Instead, I turned my fury to the only logical place it belongs in a household, the one person who had nothing to do with it – Husband.

I whirled to face him. He cradled the kitchen-floor ham in his arms. "Just cook it!" I said through clenched teeth.

Husband looked at me, then at the ham, then at me, then back at the ham.

He shook his head. "I can't," he whispered.

"FIX. IT." I said through clenched teeth.

"I will happily go get a new ham," he said. "Don't think any more about the ham."

So I didn't, and we successfully had fresh, new, disease-free ham for Easter dinner.

Perhaps, for future Easter dinners, we will have beef.

Lesson 15 - Taking a Dump Should Not Take Longer Than Five Minutes

May 2011

It was one of those rare, sunny spring days here in the Pacific Northwest, and Girlfriend and I had secured a few precious hours to ourselves during the school day. Babysitter had agreed to be at my house when Youngest got off the bus so that Girlfriend and I could visit some garage sales.

The deals were awesome – I got an entire box of clothes for the boys for $8, along with an incredible Playdoh set for (me) the kids. Hyped up on the joy of our freedom and finding good deals, Girlfriend and I decided to stop for lunch.

That's when my cell phone rang.

Girlfriend answered since my hands were full. It was Babysitter.

Within a few minutes, Girlfriend was upset and I was alarmed.

79

"Youngest hasn't arrived home from school yet," she said.

Granted, this sounded serious. But at least twice during the kindergarten school year, there had been some confusion regarding the bus not arriving on time and whatnot, so I wasn't overly concerned. I was sure that a phone call to the school would clear it up, and dialed the number to the front office.

"Oh, yeah," said the secretary. "Your son missed the bus. He's here in Afternoon kindergarten, having a great time. Can you come and pick him up?"

"How did he miss the bus?" I asked, immediately suspicious.

"Well, it appears that he went to the bathroom about ten minutes before school let out, and it was right at the end of the zoo visit assembly so everything was chaotic."

Okay, I thought. *Makes sense.*

"Then he came back to class about 11:25 and asked where all the bus riders had gone, so the teacher just had him stay."

So my son had gone to the bathroom at 10:50 and didn't come back to class until 11:25, which is when he usually gets off the bus at home.

I hung up the phone and couldn't help but laugh. Really, really hard.

"What?" Girlfriend asked. After I explained what had happened, she said, "Well, he IS a notoriously long pooper."

This is true. It's not unheard of for him to take 30 minutes to take a dump, only to become frustrated when his legs fall asleep from sitting on the toilet for so long. We dread the phrase, "I have to go poop," when we are out in public, because he takes so freakin' long to get 'er done.

But how do you explain this to those responsible for him at school? The same way, as the corny joke goes, two porcupines have sex – *very carefully*. Kindergarten Teacher was understandably chagrined, but considering my own embarrassments involving Youngest over the last couple of years, I felt like I could afford to extend some grace.

And, if I had to guess, I'm pretty confident that Youngest wasn't encouraged to poop at school for the remainder of the school year.

Lesson 16 - Don't Wear Mascara to the School Program

June 2011

I don't cry in public.

If I can at all help it, I'd rather pass out from the effort of holding in the crying than to actually just cry in front of people – my cry-face is not attractive.

One beautiful June morning, I attended Youngest's Kindergarten Program, similar to preschool or kindergarten graduation and it. Was. Adorable.

As I perched precariously on an undersized chair to watch the program, I felt an undeniable sense of accomplishment as well as an overwhelming sense of relief – I had made it through the year of kindergarten with Youngest!

I could feel my shoulders relax as I looked around the room. Kindergarten Teacher had hung up the students' art and writing projects, lending a colorful air to the celebration. Parents crowded around undersized tables clustered around the back of the classroom, with standing room only along the rear wall.

The room grew silent as the kindergarteners grouped together at the front of the room to start the program. First they performed a story, and then recited a poem that incorporated each letter of the alphabet.

I felt delighted and surprised as Youngest said his rehearsed line. I had resigned myself to the expectation that he would probably resist in some way, but only in public during the program itself.

I also noted with some alarm that not only was I on the edge of actually shedding tears, I was *choking them down*.

This strategy worked until the little kindergarten cherubs began to sing *You Are My Sunshine*.

I sang that song to my kids since they were newly born, and since my children both almost died and I consider them little miracles, it's an especially emotional song for me. I thought I could hold it together, especially with one verse, but then they were on the second verse, and by the third verse, I basically turned into a puddle.

I clawed my way through the crowded kindergarten classroom to the door, and across the hall to the women's bathroom. Girlfriend, seeing me from the back of the room, followed me.

"Are you alright?" she asked.

I stood in a locked bathroom stall, tissue jammed against my face. "I *can't believe* I wore mascara today," I said. The tissue was black from where I had pressed it against my eyes.

We laughed. Which is generally what I do basically all the time, but especially when I'm crying.

Granted, I had gotten that mascara for free from Nameless Cosmetic Company, but it wasn't waterproof, which I should have noticed while I was getting ready – but still, shouldn't every mascara be waterproof? Is there someone out there who insists on mascara smudges underneath her eyes?

Girlfriend and I stood in the bathroom for a while, while I tried to breathe and calm the panic in my chest. It was like I was crying not just because my children are growing up so fast, but for a wide range of reasons – that I had been in so much pain for at least a year, that I still hurt from a recent surgery, that Steve Carell (as Michael Scott) had left *The Office*, that the week before had marked the fifth anniversary of the death of my father-in-law, that I was frightened because being in my mid-thirties leaves a ton of time for things to go terribly wrong, and more.

I feel like I've lived a lifetime of grief in three and a half decades, and I have to say that I consider myself a bit of a specialist when it comes to loss.

But geez, mascara on kindergarten program day? Rookie mistake.

It appears that I'm going to need to find some coupons for new mascara. This time, I will make sure it's waterproof.

Lesson 17 - God's Timing is Perfect

July 2011

God provides special observational lessons regarding poop, especially when you look for them.

Each summer, I purposely search out Vacation Bible School programs in my area, and there are a couple that my kids really enjoy year after year. I also volunteer with a Vacation Bible School program at a local church, hanging out and teaching a small group of kids of elementary school age for about three hours a day during a week in the summer.

Generally, there's a special teaching time where my Teaching Partner for the week and I present some special lesson regarding Jesus specifically and spirituality in general.

The theme of one particular week involved questions about God and Jesus respectively, so I naturally wanted to ask some questions of my own without putting everyone into a bored stupor.

"So, we've been talking about questions," I said to the fifth graders sitting with me in a circle in our class area, which consisted of a cleared bit of forest right outside the church building. "And presumably when we go to Heaven, we'll be able to ask questions of Jesus."

Looking around at their faces, I could tell they were tracking with me. Teaching Partner looked *a little* nervous, I think because she knew that I was such a fan of talking about grief, didn't know where I was going with this line of thought, knew about my quirky sense of humor, and had just mentioned death and the afterlife to a group of fifth graders.

"So here's my first question," I continued. "Did Jesus actually poop?"

Kids started to snicker, which is to be expected. Honestly, though, I was completely serious.

"Think about it for a minute," I said. "Jesus was fully human, right? But He was also God's son, so if he wanted to, he could totally not poop."

"He could just skip it," someone said.

"Or it could smell good, like apple pie," someone else volunteered.

"Exactly!" I answered in the midst of the giggles. "So in light of this idea, what other questions might you want to ask Jesus?"

"Oh my word!" Teaching Partner exclaimed.

All heads in the circle swiveled in her direction.

"Is everything okay?" I asked.

"Something just pooped on me!"

All eyes stared at her.

"No!" I said. "That did not just happen!"

Teaching Partner pointed to her leg, and about an inch below the hem of her shorts, there was a brown blob. "I'm not kidding!" she said. "Poop just fell from the sky and landed on me!"

Teaching Partner stared at her leg as if she had been bitten by a snake while the rest of us tried to stop giggling. Our smirks turned to guffawing as Teaching Partner started laughing with us. Needless to say, the lesson was postponed for several minutes while we all laughed.

Later, I wondered how we should interpret this sign from above, and all I could really think was that I couldn't have planned that better if I had tried. That was perfect timing at its finest. But one thing's for sure, that blob didn't smell at all like apple pie.

Lesson 18 - There's a Good Reason Why Mom Doesn't Play Sports with You

August 2011

If you've ever studied a rock wall, then you know that it seems relatively harmless, especially when it is located at the local indoor water park.

In a fit of desperation for something to do with the kids over the summer combined with online bargain shopping, I had purchased an admittedly great deal for four admissions to the local aquatic park. This half-priced deal included a trip up the rock wall and unlimited swimming for each person.

Other moms – probably those who take issue with the title of this lesson – play sports of all kinds with their kids. I am not that mom. I'm not known for my physical prowess. Most of my adolescence included some sprain or injury of some kind in one or more appendages at a time. I never played catch because I would simply get hit in the face with the ball (this really happened). When I was in high school, I sprained my ankle when stepping out of a van to take a hike. I was on my high school freshman volleyball team for two years in a row, and I was an excellent student.

Recently, a thawing pork loin slid out of the freezer onto my ankle and foot, causing them both to bruise and swell. As Seth Meyers so accurately stated once on a *Saturday Night Live Weekend Update*, "You don't become a comedian by being good at sports."

When I "swim," the thrashing resembles someone who is drowning, so I just focus on gliding around and not unduly alarming the lifeguards.

I managed to wait until about three days before the passes expired to use them. Husband, Oldest, Youngest and I entered the aquatic park, the wave pool spreading out before us like so much used hot dog water, and the chlorine in the air frizzed my straight hair and turned the whites of my eyes a very attractive shade of bloodshot-pink. On our left, the rock wall stretched from floor to ceiling in a show of bumpy innocence.

Which might be partly why, when Oldest and Youngest pleaded with me to climb the rock wall, I couldn't resist. Usually terrible at anything that requires spatial intelligence and balance, I still like to exercise and try new things and honestly, the rock wall didn't look that hard to climb. Plus, I wanted to encourage them to try new things too, especially when said activities make you feel a little scared.

So we stood in line, and Husband went ahead of me. He's a delicate flower, so he had to stop and get his shoes because the fake rocks on the wall hurt his feet. Since this rock wall was at an aquatic center, a bathing suit and bare feet were all that was required for climbing (this should have been my first clue that this was a bad idea, seriously). *Whatever*, I thought while suiting up with the provided safety gear, *I can do this without my shoes.*

As the staffer made sure I was buckled in to the harness, Husband had returned with his shoes and was about halfway up the wall. Oldest and Youngest were next in line, waiting to get into their own harnesses.

I started up the rock wall, the hard plastic digging into the soles of my feet. Those innocent-looking nubs gouged into my tender skin so hard that my teeth ached.

It hurt. A lot.

I clung to the wall, trying to disassociate; *This is not me, I am not here*, I thought. I couldn't figure out how people thought this was fun, concluding that there must be a Rock Wall Climbing Flask that I didn't know about...yet.

Husband had reached the top and rung the bell, signaling his physical superiority, making his way back down in triumph and the comfort of his stupid shoes.

I got about (maybe) three or four feet off the ground and decided I had had enough of this experience. And when you're done climbing on a rock wall, you simply repel to the ground, right?

This may have been an unreasonable assumption.

I let go and leaned back a little, finding myself swinging through the air, doing a bit of a backward reverse somersault and pummeling into Youngest, who was getting ready to put on his harness. I was happy to land, although I was flat on my back on the mat in front of my family and easily twenty strangers surrounding the wall. And all of this while wearing my bathing suit.

Awesome.

"MOM!" Youngest yelled, not really happy with me pushing him out of the way. I tried to explain what had happened but gave up, apologizing – he hadn't seen it coming, and it was too hard to explain.

Oldest saw the whole thing, though, and asked me if I was embarrassed.

"You know," I said, "this kind of stuff happens to me *all the time*. Which is mostly why I don't play sports. And when it happens - I just laugh."

Like I quoted, you don't become funny by being good at sports.

Lesson 19 - Children Belong in the Church Basement

August 2011

Whoever decided that children should sit in the sanctuary with the adults during a church service on Sunday morning either has a pointedly cruel sense of humor or is certifiably insane.

Otherwise, why would kids be allowed to sit with us during Sunday Service at all? One of reasons that mothers go to church is for the hour of free daycare (yes, this is a terrible sentiment that no mother would freely admit, but it's true). Sitting in church without kids should be the reward for actually arriving on a Sunday morning with everyone present and fully clothed.

Why allow older kids to sit with adults in church when younger kids are prohibited? That's the whole purpose for what is known in many churches as The Nursing Room (also known as The Mother's Room).

When my babies were really little, I loved coming to church every Sunday for one reason: The Mother's Room. The sign on this door forbade entry by anyone not feeding a little baby, which limited distractions from the baby's older busy toddler siblings as well as any tasks that required completion at home – in other words, the mountains of dirty dishes and laundry piled around the house were out of my sight, at least temporarily.

Instead, there was dim lighting, comfortable rocking chairs and recliners, a couch in the corner, and fleece blankets. The door in the back of this semi-private sanctuary led to a small bathroom. It was warm. Peaceful. Quiet.

Given enough food, I could happily live there. Alone.

It was totally worth having kids in order to be able to sit in The Mother's Room, but it's an exaggeration to say that I "sat." To be honest, it was a sprawl, and generally on the couch in the corner.

As Oldest and Youngest developed through their respective toddler stages, I would stop in to The Mother's Room to "check on friends," but then just end up using the bathroom and falling asleep on the couch. To this day, I feel a sense of overwhelming fatigue and the urge to pee at the beginning of a church service.

As Oldest and Youngest have grown older, I've discovered that fellow mothers have become aware of my unlawful presence in The Mother's Room, proceeding to stare at me and judge me while I've napped. I eventually had to stop ducking in there. Instead, I began to enjoy my hour of relative peace in the back of the sanctuary, covering my ears and rocking back and forth.

Until, one fateful Sunday morning, there was no Kid's Program.

The Kid's Program at our church is the place we take our children as we arrive on Sunday morning after fighting with them in the car, picking them up once Sunday Service is over. I have noticed that in many local churches that Kid's Programs occur in the far-off corners of church campuses or in church basements. All the best churches have basements, because the builders understood that this is where the children belong on a Sunday morning.

It's not that I dislike the idea of Oldest and Youngest participating in spiritual education with Husband and me each week. The idea of children in a church service is philosophically sound but, in practice, is completely insane. Unless the purpose is to drive parents crazy – then, it's totally working.

First, my children are unable to sit still in a church service. The pews must be lined with an invisible, undetectable herb, like catnip, but for kids, that causes them to be unable to stand or sit for any length of time. The presence of this herb causes my children to spin around, roll on the floor, lie on the pew, try to jump over the pew, make faces at one another, speak in any volume but a whisper, and punch and tickle each other.

There's really little that parents can do to children who act like caged raccoons during a church service. Kids in this situation have all the power, because odds are that you don't act in church like you do at home, and your kids know it. There's no yelling at your kids during Sunday Service.

Instead, there's a progressively helpless set of tactics for parents like me who need to discipline their kids in church.

First, I give Oldest and Youngest the Eye-Twitch-and-Frozen-Smile combo, generally during the singing portion of Sunday Service. This is closely followed by the Forced Side Hug – you can tell it's forced because the knuckles clutching their shoulders or arms are white with the effort of self-control.

After Forced Side Hug – or at any time during this process - comes Clenched Teeth Talking, which is basically saying everything through teeth clenched in frustration while trying to whisper. Generally, the phrase used is "Stop. It." The children giggle.

The last step in this process before actually leaving the church service altogether is the Hand-On-Shoulder-Push-Down. This involves me placing a hand on one of my child's shoulders, forcing him into a sitting position on the pew and effectively holding him there.

Who exactly benefits spiritually from the presence of children in a Sunday Service?

Nobody.

Which is why children belong in the church basement, and a mother's prayer as we roll into the parking lot on Sunday morning is *Dear God, let there be a kid's program today.*

Lesson 20 – When in Doubt, Flush It

October 2011

There's a distinct difference between a child who's screaming when playing and one who screams because something is wrong.

One of the reasons we chose to buy our current house was that we wanted to be "that" house in the neighborhood – the one where kids come over and play after school once homework is done as well as during those "boring" weekend afternoons. The house where you can hear the yelling and screaming as children play, with bikes, scooters, and helmets piled at the side of the driveway.

Once I started working from home, our wish was granted. On any given afternoon, I had at least three additional kids running around who didn't belong to me – I loved it.

Our house is popular in part because of the space provided by the large basement, full of old furniture that can be jumped on and over, easily transformed into forts with a few carefully placed blankets and pillows. Most of the time, things tend to go wonderfully.

Most of the time.

When I heard Oldest's Friend scream in the basement bathroom one particular afternoon, I jumped up and ran for the stairs.

The kids met me at the halfway point, yelling "There's ain the toilet, there's a mouse in the toilet!!!"

"WHAT?" I asked, simultaneously considering and dismissing the chances that this could be a joke. That scream was real.

"OK, let's go down there," I said. "Wait!" I scrambled back up the stairs. "I need my camera."

So my two boys, their three friends, my camera, and I tromped down to the basement and into the rarely-used bathroom toward the apparently rarely-flushed toilet.

To my immediate disgust and fascination, I found they had been correct – there was a mouse floating in the middle of the toilet bowl. The mouse drifted in the distinct "dead man's" style - face down, four paws splayed out diagonally from each other, its tail straight out behind - in water the distinct shade of a delightfully cheerful rubber duck.

Like I said, the "rarely-flushed" toilet.

Now, had it been a fish, I would have flushed it right down without hesitation. The chances of a fish being in our toilet bowl, should we ever purchase them, are quite high, since I have a tough time keeping silk plants alive. But this -

This was a mouse.

I wasn't entirely sure about the disposal etiquette involving a mouse that wasn't in a trap. It wasn't a pet mouse, so I didn't feel the need for a funeral, per se. This mouse had paid the ultimate price, but it had also violated my home and tried to swim in the toilet (which brings me to another valuable point for kids to learn early – in nature, stupid things die). I had no intention of fishing the unwanted guest out of the (unflushed) toilet.

Plus, this was clearly a job for Husband, who with Oldest and Youngest had baited and checked mousetraps over the previous summer with a little more delight than I had appreciated. Each pleasantly warm evening, I heard chuckles of anticipation as they

102

filled each trap with a small amount of peanut butter; every sunny morning, the patter of feet to the garage and, on those lucky mornings, subsequent squeals of delight upon finding their prey.

"Dad! Dad! We got one!" Oldest and Youngest screamed from the open garage door.

Once Husband made his way to the traps, they bent close to the unlucky victim, noses centimeters from the sprung trap. Then, all together, they disposed of their quarry unceremoniously into the garbage can outside the garage.

While not in a trap, this mouse clearly needed to be disposed of, and I wasn't about to do it. I snapped a picture, closed the toilet lid, and turned to the five young faces with me in the bathroom.

"We gotta wait for Dad to get home," I said. "Everyone out. Stay out."

They happily agreed, and requested that I post the photo on Facebook – which I did, of course. When Husband arrived, six excited voices and a dog met him at the top of the stairs, clamoring about the Toilet Mouse in the basement.

"Seriously?" he asked, and went down to investigate.

About 30 seconds later, I heard the toilet flush.

"You just flushed it?" I asked when he returned to the living room.

"Sure," he said. "The rule is, if the mouse doing the dead man's float in the toilet bowl is about the size of a turd…you can flush it."

For future reference, no funeral required, and when in doubt, flush.

Lesson 21 - Don't Steal Chocolate, Especially From Your Mother

December 2011

As a parent, I often feel that the bulk of my time, effort, energy, and the words that I say are simply to manage Oldest and Youngest. This reality can be exhausting.

It was particularly tiring right around the Christmas holidays, when I bought the chocolate chips. Since the holiday season was upon us, I had taken advantage of store specials and manufacturer coupons to get a smokin' deal on those little nuggets of sweet sanity. I hid them carefully in the very top of the freezer, shoved toward the back where I presumed I would be the only one who knew of their delicious presence.

Apparently, I was wrong.

Over the course of a few days, I noticed first that one of the bags was open. Then I used some for a recipe. The next time I stuck my paw into the already-opened bag of chocolate chips, I noticed that even more of them were missing.

As I often do in the privacy of my own mind, I blamed Husband for the rapidly decreasing number of chocolate chips. He can essentially eat whatever he wants and not gain an ounce, so he can sneak on the candy with basically no consequences, whereas if I did that, I'd immediately gain at least a pound. But I digress.

To add to my general feeling of (bitter) irritation, I didn't want the chocolate chips to be eaten because I had bought them at a great price to use in a recipe especially for the Christmas holiday.

"Dude, seriously," I said once we were in the house at the same time (a rarity in the month of December). "You gotta slow down on the chocolate chips."

"What are you talking about?" Husband asked.

"Basically, I'm saying stop eating the chocolate chips because I need them for my Christmas recipe."

"But I haven't eaten any of them," he said.

"Seriously?"

"Nope."

"Hm," I replied, thinking for a moment. I had no reason to believe that he would lie, especially about chocolate chips. I considered a couple of options – #1) call the kids in and go through the whole rigamarole of who's been eating them and who's lying and all of that, or B) I could find another way because to be completely honest, I was tired of talking.

So I decided to write the following note:

Looking for the chocolate chips?

They are gone because someone or people have been sneaking them.

Sneaking food is the same as telling a lie.

Lying is wrong.

Tell your mom or dad about your sneaking chocolate chips right now.

I placed this note in the freezer in place of the chocolate chips that were once there. I wanted it to seem like the Voice of God in written form, coming out of nowhere and everywhere all at once in a tone that would make their stomachs jump and their bowels turn to water. I taped a chocolate chip to the top of the note, which is basically the same as the guy who found a horse's head in his bed in *The Godfather*.

I was a little worried about it, because I knew I ran the risk of what Ralphie in *A Christmas Story* says after his friend gets his tongue stuck to the metal pole at recess, "Kids know it's always better not to get caught." I could only hope the note held just the right amount of guilt without any lasting negative consequences – I thought this was a pretty safe possibility.

At some point during the day, I heard the freezer door open, and then close. Later, Oldest – clearly embarrassed - apologized for sneaking the chocolate chips. I had a sneaking suspicion that Youngest had been involved, but I had no proof aside from the too-innocent look on his face.

At least Oldest and I had a good talk about it. I was simply relieved to not be the only one talking this time.

Lesson 22 - Life is About Doing Stuff You Don't Want To Do

January 2012

The winter season for many people in the United States means snow. However, we generally don't have snow where we live, so we drive about an hour and a half up to the nearest mountain to have some fun playing in cold, white drifts.

When Oldest and Youngest were old enough to stand up and balance on skis, we introduced our kids to the wildly reasonable sport of skiing – who wouldn't want to strap slick boards to their kids' feet and push them down the side of a mountain?

Skiing for a family is an expensive proposition, especially when one parent is a musician and the other is a writer. There's the cost of the equipment, lessons, lift tickets, sno-park pass, whatever food you eat should you choose to purchase it, and the gas money to get up there. I was always looking for family skiing deals for the few times (okay, once) during the season that we went, and I had found an option that generally worked for our budget.

The kids were looking forward to one of our cheap ski trips when, after reviewing the budget, Husband and I decided that it wasn't going to be financially possible to go that day, especially if we wanted to live within our means. It was a good lesson for us, and I figured it would be a good one for our boys as well.

But it was a tough decision, and Husband and I were disappointed. Youngest was fine with our choice, but Oldest really had a tough time processing it. Although he was technically eight years old at the time, he could whine and produce temper tantrums to rival the brattiest toddler. This was annoying.

So finally, after listening to his disappointed ravings without squashing his spirit, my ears grew tired of the complaining and whining.

"You know what?" I said. "Life is full of things you don't want or don't get to do. I understand that our decision is disappointing, but your dad and I are trying to teach you what it means to be financially responsible. So suck it up, because I promise you that this is the least disappointing thing you'll encounter in your lifetime."

That pretty much cut off the whining, and we continued to the park for some free family fun.

The sun was relatively warm and we could even gaze upon blue sky, which we hadn't seen in weeks. Our dog ran around the dog park while the boys headed over to the play structure to blow off some steam.

At one point, Oldest ran up to Husband and me, where we sat on a bench, talking. "Mom," he said, "I'm sorry I was whining about not being able to go skiing."

"I really appreciate that," I said. "You have no idea what it means to me to hear you say that."

And he ran off, screaming (in a good way).

I sat back, stunned, and realized that I might start crying. As a mom, I don't get a lot of moments that I can point to and say, *Yep, what I'm doing is making a difference*, so I certainly treasured this one. But it also reminded me that there is financial power to saying the word "No" when it's necessary – when buying something or going somewhere will overstretch the budget.

And truly, as my own journey through parenthood strongly suggests, this clearly was not going to be the most disappointing news that my children would have to deal with.

Lesson 23 – Don't Run in the Dog Park

February 2012

It started with an innocent lick.

Our local dog park is ideal in that it's situated in the middle of a much larger piece of acreage, with a play structure about twenty yards away.

I don't particularly like our children to join us in the fenced in area where dogs of all sizes run free. The kids head to the play structure while I take Gilly, our Border Collie-Lab mix, to run around. While I can see the children, I can't *hear* them, ensuring both their safety and my sanity.

However, after they've run around for awhile, the kids love to join us in order to pet the dogs, and this fateful day, there were a couple of clumsy, floppy, adorable puppies.

Oldest and Youngest pet and cuddled and played with the puppies, but the boys did not chase them. If there's any rule that must be followed, it is, "You do not run in the dog park."

Children who run in the dog park make me nervous. They act a little too much like prey and the dogs, with their slimy, sharp teeth, look a bit too much like they might, at any moment, eat my children. So on every trip to take Gilly to play, I ask, "What's the rule?" and they answer, "You don't run in the dog park."

With this rule firmly established, the boys patiently waited for the puppies to circulate back over to where they stood, which also meant that other dogs got their fair share of petting as well. One particularly shaggy, chocolate brown, rather large dog approached Youngest.

"Whoa! He's huge!" Oldest yelled.

I had to agree. The top of his friendly brown head hit the bottom of Youngest's chin. Shaggy Brown Dog simply had to angle his cute face up a little in order to lick Youngest from said chin to forehead.

Which is what Shaggy Brown Dog did.

"UGH! BLECH!" Youngest said as Husband, Oldest and I giggled.

"Come!" Shaggy Brown Dog's owner said. "Over here! Go run."

Shaggy Brown Dog took off, only to wander back to Youngest. It seemed he had taken quite a shine to Youngest, because this time he reared up, placed his paws on Youngest's shoulders, and licked him again from chin to forehead.

"AAAAGGGHHH! AAAAGGGHHH!" Youngest yelled.

The owner and I both commanded the dog to get down, which he did, chasing another dog around the field. Youngest was emoting in the fashion that I like to call "Yell-Crying." He was a little frightened, but there were no tears.

This incident may seem like enough motivation to pack everyone up and go, but it was a beautiful day and Gilly, at least, was having a great time. We hadn't been there very long, and after several years of experience with dogs, I've cultivated a sense about them. Shaggy Brown Dog, while romantically charged and a little overzealous, was basically harmless.

Oldest and Youngest were surrounded by the puppies and a couple of smaller dogs when Shaggy Brown Dog sidled over. He made to rear up again, but Youngest turned his back and – quite calmly, I thought – moved out of reach.

At least, he tried. Since he had been forbidden to run in the dog park, he didn't move nearly as fast as he needed to.

Shaggy Brown Dog took Youngest's turned back as an invitation, rearing up, placing both paws on Youngest's shoulders, and essentially mounting him. Youngest, hunkered forward, yelled for help while Shaggy Brown Dog proceeded to try and…well…hump him.

Youngest folded beneath the weight of Shaggy Brown Dog, but the dog wasn't deterred. Husband, Shaggy Brown Dog's Owner, and I crowded around while Youngest was pushed into the soft, oozing mud.

Shaggy Brown Dog's Owner stared at me, alarmed, while I guffawed and yelled for the dog to get off my son. I got the sense that he thought I was crazy. I think I might have been temporarily insane.

I now intimately understand the true meaning of the word "hysteria," and its equally alarming cousin, "hysterical." At that moment, I experienced such a potent combination of absolute terror and sheer gut-busting laughter that I thought it might literally kill me.

Youngest turned over as Shaggy Brown Dog was pulled away, and the puppies ran over, clearly thinking that it was time to play.

I guess they didn't hear Youngest yelling and crying as they proceeded to jump all over him.

Peripherally, I could see the owner leaving the dog park with Shaggy Brown Dog as we helped Youngest up from the mud and the crowd of interested and possibly scandalized dog owners dispersed. We walked Youngest over to the nearest bench.

"Waaaaaaaahhh," he cried, a bit half-heartedly. "STOP LAUGHING!" he yelled at Oldest and me.

"Fair enough," I said, trying to breathe and calm my heart down to a more reasonable amount of beats-per-minute. "I'm just really scared. I'm sorry."

"Don't you get it?" Youngest yelled at me. "I could have DIED."

Husband and I looked at each other…and burst into laughter.

It was either that, or cry.

Lesson 24 – Impulse Giving is Good

March 2012

On our latest annual trip to Chuck E. Cheese, we stopped at the end of the exit ramp because the light was red. This particular intersection has routinely been populated by a variety of Sign Holders for as long as I can remember (granted, since I had children, my long-term memory has been severely affected).

Sign Holders are the people seen on the side of the road holding signs that say a combination of *God Bless, Cheap Work/Will Work for Cheap, Anything Helps*, that kind of thing, and are, I assume, homeless.

Today was no different, in that both sides of the intersection was populated by one Sign Holder each. Although I considered using the center lane, I needed to turn left. I reluctantly stopped in the left lane, but I pulled up so I could only see the Sign Holder (*Veteran/Work Cheap*) out of my peripheral vision.

I'm not proud of this. I am ashamed.

Frankly, homeless people scare me, including Sign Holders. When faced with one, I have no idea what to do, and I become paralyzed with indecision. My occasional work with homeless people in the past has taught me that many suffer with mental or physical illness and have been displaced by a lack of state funding. My American capitalist background tells me that people need to pull themselves up by their bootstraps and they'll just use any money I give them for drugs or alcohol. Jesus tells me in the Bible to clothe and feed those in need.

So instead of stroking out from this jumble of thoughts and emotions, I just pull my car as far forward as I can in the intersection and avoid eye contact.

But because I pulled so far forward, Youngest and Oldest had full visual access to the Sign Holder.

"If I wanted a sandwich and I had money for two sandwiches, then I would buy two sandwiches and give him one," Youngest said.

"That sounds like a good idea," Oldest said. "You could drive around with your car full of sandwiches, then just hand them out."

"Why is he out there?" Youngest asked. "It says he will work cheap."

"Well, I really don't know," I said. "It looks like he's homeless."

Oldest, always the detailed, rational one, asked, "Where did he get the folding chair?"

The light turned green and I headed through the intersection. "Not sure," I said. "Could be that someone gave it to him. He had a cane, so I don't think he's comfortable standing."

They considered this while I continued. "I've learned that many homeless people are mentally or physically disabled and unable to care for themselves. The state used to take care of them but when funding is cut, then people are out on the street for a variety of reasons."

Chuck E. Cheese loomed on our left. I turned into the parking lot and pulled into a space.

"So, can we get him a sandwich?" Youngest asked.

"You want to?" I admit, I was stalling, conscious of the fact that this was a critical moment. I didn't want to blow my chance to teach my kids something really valuable about giving to others no matter how afraid I might be.

I remembered a phrase the pastor at my church said recently. "We may have to control our impulse to consume, but we never have to question the impulse to give to those in need."

As a frugal person, I internalized this phrase to consider over time, and it has been my experience that he was exactly right.

"Yes!" they both said. "Let's get him a sandwich!"

"Okay," I said, putting the car in drive and pulling out of the parking space. "I don't know where a grocery store is around here, but there's a McDonald's right there. Should we get a gift card?"

"Why?" Oldest asked.

"Maybe he's not hungry right now, but he can use it later. I've got five bucks in my wallet," I offered. "Plus, we don't know what kind of food he really likes from McDonald's."

Youngest and Oldest agreed that this was a good idea, so we went inside to purchase the gift card. We walked the short distance back to the intersection where we saw the Sign Holder, Youngest skipping along the sidewalk while Oldest and I walked and chatted.

We slowed down as we approached. The man huddled inside his coat, perched on the edge of the crooked folding chair.

We stopped right behind him, unsure as to how to proceed. I felt like a child myself – shy, slightly embarrassed, and wanting to help.

He turned around and saw us, and we said hi, handing him the gift card. The traffic passing by made it hard to hear him, but he and the boys exchanged words of "thank you" and "you're welcome."

As we turned away, I felt my heart break.

I tried to process this feeling as I sat at in a red vinyl booth in the middle of Chuck E. Cheese, surrounded with the constant bleeping and flashing lights from various machines. This trip requires a flask, but of course I don't bring one with me on the once-a-year pilgrimage we make for a few hours of family entertainment.

While sapping me of sanity through the endless onslaught of noise and additional stimulus, a trip to Chuck E. Cheese serves as a special form of bribery for a long-term good behavior plan with both Oldest and Youngest.

This time, though, it felt surreal – how in moments we could go from heartbreaking sadness and a feeling of helplessness to a life-sized plastic mouse, tarnished tokens and the unending cacophony of synthesized sound.

Confused and a little angry, I was poised for any whining from the children as they ran back and forth from the games to the table where I sat. They dumped their tickets and counted their coins, ate some pizza and played on the indoor jungle gym. There was no complaining, so I put my righteous anger and lectures about gratefulness away for another day.

Oldest and Youngest seemed to have no confusion regarding the two worlds they had straddled, as evidenced by the chatter in the van on the way home. They reviewed their experiences and asked more questions, moving seamlessly between talking about fun at Chuck E. Cheese and exploring why people are homeless.

Neither Oldest nor Youngest seemed to be bothered by the juxtaposition of these two worlds, they had simply observed a need and responded.

Which, to my great benefit, included buying a sandwich for a homeless man.

Lesson 25 – Don't Steal from Jesus

April 2012

Our weekly bible study was in the classrooms of a Christian School located in a church basement (where, as you may recall, is where children belong while at church).

These classrooms were graciously loaned to us for free to use during our bible study time, and I imagined that teachers who used these rooms on a regular basis wanted to keep everything stored inside them.

Youngest disagreed.

One evening as we were leaving bible study, he produced a small eraser from his pocket. It was about the size of a half-dollar and in the shape of a soccer ball.

"Nice," I said. "Where'd you get that?"

He looked up at me, tossing the eraser from hand to hand as we walked. "From class," he said.

He was a little too casual for my taste. "Which class?"

"At school."

"Oh, cool! Did First Grade Teacher give it to you?"

"Ummmm, nn – yes," he said.

"Well," I said, sensing that I had caught Youngest in my web, "I'll have to email him a thank you."

Youngest stopped in the middle of the church parking lot. "Actually…my friend gave it to me."

"Uh huh," I said. "Seriously, where'd you get it? Don't lie to me."

He studied my face, then his shoulders slumped. "Bible study."

"Did the teacher give it to you?"

He shook his head.

"So you just took it from the classroom."

He nodded.

I pointed toward the entrance to the church. "Let's go."

I marched Youngest back down to the church basement so that he could apologize to his teacher.

125

"Thank you, Youngest," she said once Youngest explained himself and returned the eraser. "It's really important that we not take things that don't belong to us."

Youngest nodded with innocent eyes.

I fumed. *That's it?* I thought as we headed back toward the car. *Now what?*

As we buckled in and I started the car, I flipped the rear-view mirror down. "Really? Stealing from bible study?"

His face remained impassive as our eyes met in the mirror.

"Do you really want to…to…steal from Jesus?" I said, my frustration bubbling over. "Do you really think this is a wise move? Have your retained no information about Jesus?"

"What's 'retained'?" Youngest asked.

I ignored the question. "I mean, this is the guy who won an argument with the devil after wandering the desert for 40 days and nights, plus totally got pounded with nails. Do you want a piece of that?" I asked. "Seriously, the DUDE ROSE FROM THE DEAD!"

Youngest looked a little frightened at this point, maybe due to the passionately loud volume of my voice and the crazy glint in my eye.

"Don't. Steal. From. Jesus." I said, flipping the rear view mirror back into position.

The drive home was quiet.

"Room," I said to Youngest as we arrived home.

"What's going on?" Husband asked as Youngest marched to his room and closed the door.

I sighed and sat next to him in the living room, briefly explaining the situation.

"So let me understand this," Husband said. "Youngest stole something from a classroom located inside a church and then, when asked about it, lied to you?"

"Correct.

"That's two commandments broken in the space of, what? Five minutes?"

"Also correct," I said.

"Don't steal from Jesus?" he asked.

I smiled. "I got nothing else."

He smiled back. "And bible study is really helping us out here."

Lesson 26 - Don't Tell Stupid Lies

May 2012

What I didn't tell Mr. Principal when he called in February 2012 was that there was an excellent reason why Youngest was so forthcoming with the truth on the day he punched two kids in the junk. Basically, he's not a very good liar – perhaps he just didn't want to go through the process of being called out with the principal. With me, however, he chooses to go through the progression of lying and then getting caught on a fairly regular basis.

The trampoline in our backyard was a big draw for the neighborhood kids as well as for my own. By sitting in Husband's recliner, I could sit by the window and watch the crazy acrobatics while working on my computer. While I could hear the happy screams, I couldn't necessarily make out words or conversation…until somebody cussed.

128

I had only heard a child cuss in my house once, and I wasn't even in the room. Apparently, I can hear everything that happens in the basement bathroom from the master bathroom right above, and I heard this sweet little high-pitched voice say "shit" during a spirited round of hide and seek.

The judgment from the other children, I was happy to hear, was swift and final. The indignant yells pointed toward this atrocity caused an immediate apology to be issued from the guilty party and, once order was restored, the game resumed.

I heard these same indignant tones when kids began yelling while jumping on the trampoline one afternoon. Recognizing the familiar tone, I looked up from my work to see Oldest marching Youngest up the stairs.

Oldest, with a strong sense of moral rectitude, looked absolutely scandalized. Youngest looked bored.

"Mom!" Oldest yelled at me from three feet away. "Youngest said the *B word*."

After a previous misunderstanding of what constituted the *F word* along with its potential definition(s), I had learned an important lesson regarding clarification during discussions concerning words of the English language. I asked the all-important question: "What *B word*?"

"You know," Oldest whispered. "Witch but not witch."

"Ah." I nodded in understanding. "Thank you. You may go."

Oldest left reluctantly, clearly enjoying the administration of justice as only a child can who hasn't yet made any major mistakes.

"So Youngest, what did you say, exactly?" I asked.

He looked around the room, hoping for a distraction. I cocked an eyebrow at him and pursed my lips.

"Weeeelll," he began, his expression leading to what I could only imagine was a fabulous and totally fabricated story.

"Don't lie to me," I said, cutting him off.

"Okay, well, somebody did a jump on the trampoline and I said it was…bitchin'," he admitted.

I arranged my expression carefully, willing each facial muscle into stillness. This took severe self-control, as hearing these particular words come from a six-year-old was unintentionally quite hilarious.

Biting the inside of my cheek, I studied his face. He appeared to tell the truth.

"Where'd you hear that word?" I asked.

"I don't know," he said. "At school or on the bus."

"Would you say this word at school?"

This time, he was the one who looked scandalized. "What? No way!"

"Then why would you say something like that at home?" I asked. "You know good and well that we don't use inappropriate words in our family."

He shrugged. I stared. He refused to squirm. I continued to stare.

"Wait," he said.

"What?"

"Well, actually, I was thinking about kitchen and then I just put the b at the front of the word instead of the k –"

"What?" I cut him off. "Seriously? Do you think I'm stupid?"

(In retrospect, I understand the foolishness of this question, and have resolved not to ask it again).

"No-o," he said, clearly not sure where I was going with this.

"Not only are you lying to me, but you are insulting my intelligence with such a stupid lie!" I said. "Do you really think I'm going to believe something like that?"

He shook his head.

"Keep in mind for the future – tell a lie, get caught. Tell a stupid lie, get caught *faster*," I said. "Room. Go. Now."

As he sat silently in his room, I had plenty of time and mental space to evaluate this conversation, which I admit was not my finest. Seriously, I was encouraging him to lie more intelligently?

That was not going to win me the Mother of the Year award.

However, I think that I had always consoled myself by pointing out that lying is, in fact, a sign of intelligence, especially since Youngest had grasped this behavior shortly after he began speaking. I had also become a fan of teaching my children how to argue using persuasive tactics and logic, which requires careful thought, and can turn whining into conversations that can be resolved.

Since I had communicated that I would not listen to stupid arguments, what followed naturally in my mind was that I wouldn't listen to stupid lies, either. This, however, didn't work for me in a moral sense.

132

Perhaps the lesson I should continue to teach is not to lie at all, since it's just basically wrong.

Seems obvious, doesn't it?

Acknowledgements

One of the most intense dichotomies I experience are the moments where I imagine my life without children, usually while envying a friend who is not a parent, but then realize that I would absolutely not be the person I am today without Oldest and Youngest. They have and continue to add joy and depth to my life, and I thank them in advance for allowing me to write about them.

I want to acknowledge the input of Jone Rush-MacCulloch, who first told me to not only write down these stories, but to put them in a book. I also thank her and my writing buddies Kathleen King-Reeves and Lisa Mills for then reading each of the stories and offering thoughtful questions and critiques through this process, all while providing excellent snacks.

I thank my friends – Christine Draper, Charlotte Kammer and Tae-Ja Griggs - who listen to my insanity and talk me down off the proverbial ledge on a regular basis, and who also offered free input and editing services for this book (so blame them for the typos).

Thanks as always to Jamie Young, who is a patient and creative computer dude who helps me with Wilson Writes – visit and see his work at www.WilsonWrites.com!

Last but of course not least, I thank Husband. When he read the first version of this book, he chuckled during certain parts and remarked, "Wow…you are just telling a lot of stories about our life."

"So what do you think?" I asked. "Should I not publish it?"

"Oh, I don't think that at all," he said. "It's great!"

Now THAT is amazing support. I thank Husband for allowing me to share more than anyone should ever be allowed to in order to illustrate our vulnerability and just plain craziness as parents, as well as providing me time alone to finish the book. I thank him for being the best husband and father in the world (I also feel sorry for every other woman in the world, unless he's managed to create a secret second family somewhere, which always happens to the unsuspecting wife on the Lifetime movie – therefore, I *always* suspect it…just to be safe).

I hope this book is, in some way, encouraging.

Or, at the very least, entertaining.

About the Author

Kelly Wilson is an author and comedian who entertains and inspires with stories of humor, healing, and hope. She is the author of *Live Cheap and Free, Don't Punch People in the Junk, Kelly Wilson's The Art of Seduction: Nine Easy Ways to Get Sex From Your Mate.* Her latest book, *Caskets From Costco*, is a finalist in the 18th annual Foreword Reviews' INDIEFAB Book of the Year Awards and has also been chosen as a finalist in the 10th annual National Indie Excellence Book Awards.

As a survivor of childhood sexual abuse, Kelly writes and speaks about finding hope in the process of recovery. Through both stand-up and improv comedy, she brings laughter to audiences of all ages using a wide range of subject matter, including silly songs, parenting stories, and jokes and anecdotes revolving around mental health issues.

Kelly Wilson currently writes for a living and lives with her Magically Delicious husband, junk-punching children, dog, cat, and stereotypical minivan in Portland, Oregon. Read more about her at http://www.wilsonwrites.com.

www.ingramcontent.com/pod-product-compliance
Lightning Source LLC
Chambersburg PA
CBHW070635030426
42337CB00020B/4019